Travel Journal
New York

VPJournals

Copyright © 2016 VPJournals

All rights reserved.

ISBN-13: 978-1518862885
ISBN-10: 1518862888

Contact Details

Name:

Email address:

Tel:

Address:

Important Medical Information

Blood type:

Medication:

CONTENTS

Hi, I hope you enjoy this journal. It is packed with cool stuff and recommendations for you trip to New York, and has plenty of space to record details of your trip.

What's Inside   Page

Before you go to New York
Great places to visit in New York	**6-7**
Cool places to visit in New York with kids	**8-9**
Good places to eat	**10-11**
Research New York	**12-13**
Postcard & Packing List	**14-19**
New York facts	**21-22**

Helpful hints   **23-26**
Clothes and shoe sizing charts, to help you get the right sizes while there

New York Trip Diary   **27-111**
21 day trip diary to record details of your trip

Reflect on you Trip
Summary of your trip	**113-121**
People you met	**123-125**

Useful Resources   **127-136**
Size conversion charts	**129-132**
Common Translations	**133-134**
Notes	**135-136**

Have fun in New York

Great Places to visit in New York

The Statue of Liberty	✓
The High Line Park, walk	
Central Park	
Metropolitan Museum of Art	
Guggenheim Museum	
The Empire State Building	
Grand Central Station	
Times Square	
Brooklyn Bridge	
Whiskey Bars	
The West Village	

9/11 Memorial	
Cony Island	
New York Transit Museum	
Top of the Rock	
Shopping – Bloomingdales, 5th Avenue	
MoMA	
Central Park Zoo	
NY Hall of Science	
Bike Across Brooklyn Bridge	
Madison Square Garden	
Yankee Stadium	
Watch a show on Broadway	

Cool Places to visit with Kids

Empire State Building	✓
Central Park	
American Museum of Natural History	
Bronx Zoo	
Brooklyn Bridge	
Citi Field	
Coney Island	
The Statue of Liberty	
Yankee Stadium	
Times Square – Toys R Us	
Wave Hill	

Top of the Rock Observation Deck	
9/11 Memorial Museum	
Grand Central Station	
Bryant Park	
Broadway	
Madison Square Gardens	
Brooklyn Children's Museum	
Bike Across Brooklyn Bridge	
Brooklyn Ice Cream Factory	
Sony Wonder Technology Lab	
Battery Park	
One World Observatory, World Trade Center	

Good Places to Eat in New York

Famous Dave's BBQ	✓
Roberta's Pizza	
Franny's Pizza	
Narcissa	
ABC Kitchen	
The Spotted Pig	
The Breslin Bar & Dining Room	
Del Posto Italian	
Osteria Morini Italian	
Keens Steakhouse	
Balthazar	

Dirty French	
The NoMad	
RedFarm	
Taqueria Coatzingo Mexican	
Lombardi's Pizza	
Absolute Bagels	
Crif Dogs hotdogs	
Shake Shack	
Clinton St. Baking Company	
Kenka Japanese	
Burger Joint	
Lincoln Square Steak	

Best Websites to Research Further

Do some more research on the internet to plan your trip:

NYCtourist.com
NYCgo.com
IloveNY.com
lonelyplanet.com/usa/new-york-city
NYC.com
NewYork.com
Nomadicmatt.com/travel-guides/united-states-travel-guide/new-york-city/
Walksofnewyork.com
Lovingnewyork.co.uk

More places I want to visit on our trip

1. _____
2. _____
3. _____
4. _____
5. _____
6. _____
7. _____
8. _____
9. _____
10. _____
11. _____
12. _____
13. _____
14. _____
15. _____

Postcard List

Name:
Address:

Name:
Address:

Name:
Address:

Name:

Address:

Name:

Address:

Name:

Address:

Name:

Address:

Name:

Address:

Name:

Address:

Name:

Address:

Name:

Address:

Name:
Address:

Name:
Address:

Name:
Address:

Packing List

✓	This Journal
	Tickets
	Passport
	Money
	Chargers
	Batteries
	Book to read
	Camera
	Tablet
	Sun glasses
	Sun cream

	Toiletries
	Water
	Watch
	Snacks
	Umbrella
	Towel
	Guide book
	Kindle
	Jacket
	Medication
	Add more below

New York Facts

- New York is the most populated city in the USA, with a population of around 8.5 million people. 36% of the population of New York City were born outside the United States

- The New York subway system is the largest mass transit system in the world with 468 stations and 842 miles of track. It runs 24 hours a day

- The NYC Marathon is the largest in the world, with over 37,000 people finishing the race each year

- Central Park attracts 25 million visitors each year

- The Metropolitan Museum of Art contains over 2 million works, making it one of the largest museum's in the world

- New York City has over 4,000 street food vendors. Selling all different types of food

- The first pizzeria in the United States was opened in NYC in 1895

- Up until 1957, there was a pneumatic mail tube system that was used to connect 23 post offices across 27 miles. It moved up to 97,000 letters a day

- The Empire State Building has its own zip code

- On 28th November 2012, not a single murder, shooting, stabbing or other violent crime in NYC was reported for an entire day. The first time there has ever been a day without a single violent crime committed

- There is a birth in NYC every 4.4 minutes, there is a death every 9.1 minutes

- NYC has the largest Puerto Rican population of any city in the world and the largest Chinese population of any city outside Asia

- It costs $1 million to get a license (medallion) to operate a taxicab

- The Jewish population in NYC is the largest in the world outside of Israel

- About 1 in every 38 people living in the US, live in NYC

Clothes & Shoe Sizes

Children's Shoe Sizes

UK	EUROPE	US	Japan
4	20	4½ or 5	12 ½
4 ½	21	5 or 5½	13
5	21 or 22	5½ or 6	13 ½
5 ½	22	6	13½ or 14
6	23	6½ or 7	14 or 14½
6 ½	23 or 24	7 ½	14½ or 15
7	24	7½ or 8	15
7 ½	25	8 or 9	15 ½
8	25 or 26	8½ or 9	16
8 ½	26	9½	16 ½
9	27	9½ or 10	16 ½ or 17
10	28	10½ or 11	17 ½
10½ or 11	29	11½ or 12	18
11 ½	30	12½	18 or 18 ½
12	31	13	19 or 19 ½
12 ½	31	13 or 13½	19 ½ or 20
13	32	1	20
13 ½	32 ½	1 ½	20 ½
1	33	1½ or 2	21
2	34	2½ or 3	22

Children's Clothing Sizes

UK	EUROPE	US	Australia
12m	80cm	12-18m	12m
18m	80-86cm	18-24m	18m
24m	86-92cm	23-24m	2
2-3	92-98cm	2T	3
3-4	98-104cm	4T	4
3-5	104-110cm	5	5
5-6	110-116cm	6	6
6-7	116-122cm	6X-7	7
7-8	122-128cm	7 to 8	8
8-9	128-134cm	9 to 10	9
9-10	134-140cm	10	10
10-11	140-146cm	11	11
11-12	146-152cm	14	12

Women's Shoe Sizes

UK	EUROPE	US	Japan
3	35 ½	5	22 ½
3 ½	36	5 ½	23
4	37	6	23
4 ½	37 ½	6 ½	23 ½
5	38	7	24
5 ½	39	7 ½	24
6	39 ½	8	24 ½
6 ½	40	8 ½	25
7	41	9 ½	25 ½
7 ½	41 ½	10	26
8	42	10 ½	26 ½

Women's Clothes Sizes

UK	US	Japan	France / Spain	Germany	New York	Australia
6/8	6	7-9	36	34	40	8
10	8	9-11	38	36	42	10
12	10	11-13	40	38	44	12
14	12	13-15	42	39	46	14
16	14	15-17	44	40	48	16
18	16	17-19	46	42	50	18
20	18	19-21	48	44	52	20

Men's Shoe Sizes

UK	EUROPE	US	Japan
6	38 ½	6 ½	24 ½
6 ½	39	7	25
7	40	7 ½	25 ½
7 ½	41	8	26
8	42	8 ½	27 ½
8 ½	43	9	27 ½
9	43 ½	9 ½	28
9 ½	44	10	28 ½
10	44	10 ½	28 ½
10 ½	44 ½	11	29
11	45	12	29 ½

Men's Suit / Coat / Sweater Sizes

UK / US / Aus	EU / Japan	General
32	42	Small
34	44	Small
36	46	Small
38	48	Medium
40	50	Large
42	52	Large
44	54	Extra Large
46	56	Extra Large

Men's Pants / Trouser Sizes (Waist)

UK / US	Europe
32	81 cm
34	86 cm
36	91 cm
38	97 cm
40	102 cm
42	107 cm

We have included another copy of this at the back of the book, so you can find it quickly again when you are in New York

New York Trip Diary
Write a daily diary during your trip

Day 1

Date: _____   **Weather:** _____

Day 2

Date: _____ **Weather:** _____

Day 3

Date: _____ **Weather:** _____

Day 4

Date: _____   **Weather:** _____

Day 5

Tip! Send your postcards

Date: **Weather:**

Day 6

Date: _____   **Weather:** _____

Day 7

Date: _____ **Weather:** _____

Day 8

Date: **Weather:**

Day 9

Date: **Weather:**

Day 10

Date: _____   **Weather:** _____

Day 11

Date: _____   **Weather:** _____

Day 12

Date: _____   **Weather:** _____

Day 13

Date: _____   **Weather:** _____

Day 14

Date: _____ **Weather:** _____

Day 15

Date: _____ **Weather:** _____

Day 16

Date: **Weather:**

Day 17

Date: _____   **Weather:** _____

Day 18

Date: _____ **Weather:** _____

Day 19

Date: _____   **Weather:** _____

Day 20

Date: _____   Weather: _____

Day 21

Date: _____ **Weather:** _____

Memories of your Trip

Things I will remember from the trip

Favorite Places visited on the Trip

People I Met

Name:
Address:
Tel:
email:

Name:
Address:
Tel:
email:

Name:
Address:
Tel:
email:

Name:
Address:
Tel:
email:

Name:
Address:
Tel:
email:

Name:
Address:
Tel:
email:

Name:
Address:
Tel:
email:

Name:

Address:

Tel:

email:

Name:

Address:

Tel:

email:

Name:

Address:

Tel:

email:

Name:

Address:

Tel:

email:

We hope you enjoyed your trip to New York

Please leave us a review if you found this Journal useful

Check out our useful resources on the next few pages

Clothes & Shoe Sizes

Children's Shoe Sizes

UK	EUROPE	US	Japan
4	20	4½ or 5	12 ½
4 ½	21	5 or 5½	13
5	21 or 22	5½ or 6	13 ½
5 ½	22	6	13½ or 14
6	23	6½ or 7	14 or 14½
6 ½	23 or 24	7 ½	14½ or 15
7	24	7½ or 8	15
7 ½	25	8 or 9	15 ½
8	25 or 26	8½ or 9	16
8 ½	26	9½	16 ½
9	27	9½ or 10	16 ½ or 17
10	28	10½ or 11	17 ½
10½ or 11	29	11½ or 12	18
11 ½	30	12½	18 or 18 ½
12	31	13	19 or 19 ½
12 ½	31	13 or 13½	19 ½ or 20
13	32	1	20
13 ½	32 ½	1 ½	20 ½
1	33	1½ or 2	21
2	34	2½ or 3	22

Children's Clothing Sizes

UK	EUROPE	US	Australia
12m	80cm	12-18m	12m
18m	80-86cm	18-24m	18m
24m	86-92cm	23-24m	2
2-3	92-98cm	2T	3
3-4	98-104cm	4T	4
3-5	104-110cm	5	5
5-6	110-116cm	6	6
6-7	116-122cm	6X-7	7
7-8	122-128cm	7 to 8	8
8-9	128-134cm	9 to 10	9
9-10	134-140cm	10	10
10-11	140-146cm	11	11
11-12	146-152cm	14	12

Women's Shoe Sizes

UK	EUROPE	US	Japan
3	35 ½	5	22 ½
3 ½	36	5 ½	23
4	37	6	23
4 ½	37 ½	6 ½	23 ½
5	38	7	24
5 ½	39	7 ½	24
6	39 ½	8	24 ½
6 ½	40	8 ½	25
7	41	9 ½	25 ½
7 ½	41 ½	10	26
8	42	10 ½	26 ½

Women's Clothes Sizes

UK	US	Japan	France / Spain	Germany	New York	Australia
6/8	6	7-9	36	34	40	8
10	8	9-11	38	36	42	10
12	10	11-13	40	38	44	12
14	12	13-15	42	39	46	14
16	14	15-17	44	40	48	16
18	16	17-19	46	42	50	18
20	18	19-21	48	44	52	20

Men's Shoe Sizes

UK	EUROPE	US	Japan
6	38 ½	6 ½	24 ½
6 ½	39	7	25
7	40	7 ½	25 ½
7 ½	41	8	26
8	42	8 ½	27 ½
8 ½	43	9	27 ½
9	43 ½	9 ½	28
9 ½	44	10	28 ½
10	44	10 ½	28 ½
10 ½	44 ½	11	29
11	45	12	29 ½

Men's Suit / Coat / Sweater Sizes

UK / US / Aus	EU / Japan	General
32	42	Small
34	44	Small
36	46	Small
38	48	Medium
40	50	Large
42	52	Large
44	54	Extra Large
46	56	Extra Large

Men's Pants / Trouser Sizes (Waist)

UK / US	Europe
32	81 cm
34	86 cm
36	91 cm
38	97 cm
40	102 cm
42	107 cm

Common Translations

English	French	Spanish	Italian
Hello	Bonjour	Hola	Ciao
Goodbye	Au revoir	Adiós	Arrivederci
Yes	Oui	Sí	Si
No	Non	No	No
Please	S'il-vous-plaît	Por favor	Per favore
Thank you	Merci	Gracias	Grazie
Excuse me	Excusez-moi	Perdón	Mi scusi
How much	Combien	Cuánto	Quanto
My name is	Mon nom est	Mi nombre es	Io mi chiamo
Where is	Où est	Dónde está	Dov'è
The bank	La banque	El banco	La banca
The toilet	Les toilettes	El baño	Il bagno

German	Japanese	Mandarin	Hindi
Hallo	Kon'nichiwa	Ni hao	Namaste
Auf Wiedersehen	Sayonara	Zaijian	Alavida
Ja	Hai	Shi de	Ham
Nein	Ie	Meiyou	Nahim
Bitte	Onegaishimasu	Qing	Krpaya
Vielen Dank	Arigato	Xiexie	Dhan'yavada
Entschuldigung	Sumimasen	Duoshao	Mujhe mapha karem
Wie viel	Ikura	Wo de mingzi shi	Kitana
Mein Name ist	Watashinonamaeha	Nali	Mera nama hai
Wo ist	Doko ni aru	Yinhang	Kaham hai
Die Bank	Ginko	Yinhang	Bainka
Die Toilette	Toire	Cesuo	Saucalaya

Notes:

Printed in Great Britain
by Amazon